WITHDRAWN

Hotchkiss Public Library
P.O. Box 540
Hotchkiss, CO 81419

APR 05

S0-DFG-771

Space

The Scribbles Institute™ *Young Artist Basics*

Published by The Child's World®
PO Box 326
Chanhassen, MN 55317-0326
800-599-READ
www.childsworld.com

Copyright © 2003 The Scribbles Institute™
All rights reserved. No part of this book may be reproduced or utilized in any form or by any means without permission from the publisher.
Printed in the United States of America

Design and Production: The Creative Spark, San Juan Capistrano, CA
Series Editor: Elizabeth Sirimarco Budd

Photos:
© Corel Corporation: cover, 10, 16-17
© CORBIS: 14
© Philip James Corwin/CORBIS: 23
© Fine Art Photographic Library, London/Art Resource, NY: 30
© Werner Forman/Art Resource, NY: 11
© Jet Propulsion Laboratory, California Institute of Technology: 2
© Erich Lessing/Art Resource, NY: 8
© 2002 Sol LeWitt/Artists Rights Society (ARS), New York/© Tate Gallery, London/Art Resource, NY: 26
© The Newark Museum/Art Resource, NY: 18-19
© 2002 Estate of Pablo Picasso/Artists Rights Society (ARS), New York/© Réunion des Musées Nationaux/Art Resource, NY: 24
© Scala/Art Resource, NY: 13
© Smithsonian American Art Museum, Washington, DC/Art Resource, NY: 28.

Library of Congress Cataloging-in-Publication Data

  Space / by Rob Court.
       p. cm. — (Young artists basics series)
Includes index.
Summary: Simple text and "Loopi the Fantastic Line" describe the concept of space in art and architecture.
  ISBN 1-56766-108-4
  1. Art—Philosophy—Juvenile literature. 2. Space (Architecture)—Juvenile literature. [1. Space (Art) 2. Space (Architecture)] I. Title. II. Series.
  N62 .C779 2002
  701'.8—dc21
                                          2002005501

Space

Rob Court

Loopi is a line,
a fantastic line.

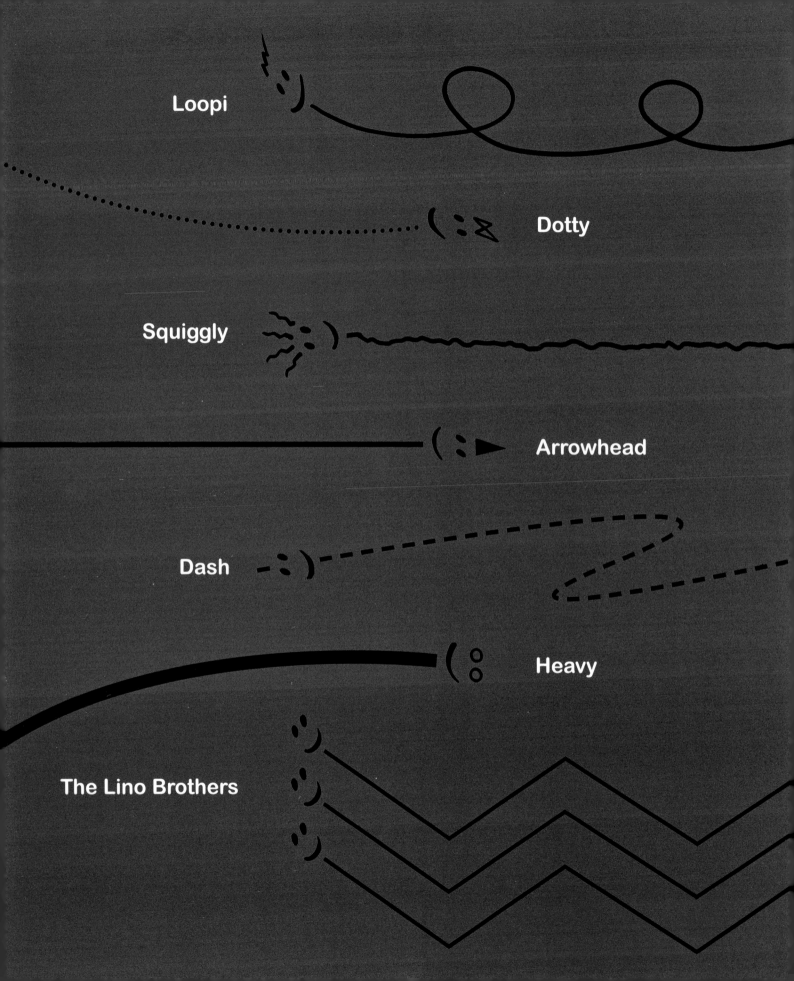

There are many kinds of lines.

Some are dotted lines.

Some are squiggly lines.

Some lines point in a direction.

Some lines are drawn with dashes.

Other lines are very, very thick.

Sometimes lines work together
to help you see space.

This cave painting was made on a flat wall. It is more than 3,000 years old! Do you see the shapes of two people and an animal? The color inside the shapes is dark red. Is there a color outside of the shapes?

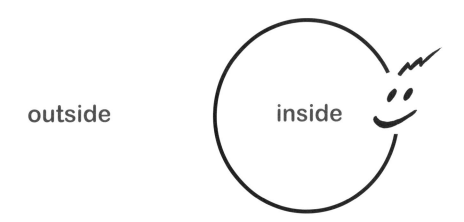

outside   inside

Loopi is making the shape of a circle. Look closely at the wall painting. Can you find big and small shapes that look like Loopi? What color is the space inside of each shape? What color is the space outside of each shape?

This is a pyramid in Egypt. It is not flat. There is space beyond the form of the pyramid. The blue space above it is the sky.

The picture to the right shows the inside of the pyramid. Do you think there is much space inside?

Squiggly shows you a small hole in the pyramid's wall that you can crawl through. Can you see the space behind the wall?

Sometimes artists create paintings, photographs, or **sculptures** of themselves. These are called self-portraits. Albrecht Dürer made this self-portrait more than 500 years ago. His work helped artists learn to create paintings that look like the real world. Dürer's painting can help you learn about space.

Can you find Loopi in Dürer's painting? Loopi helps you see the space outside the window. Can you see the sky? There are dark walls painted in the space behind Dürer's body. Is he inside or outside?

Right: Albrecht Dürer, *Self-Portrait,* 15th century. Oil on wood panel.

You can see space everywhere. The sky is the blue space above the ground. The place where the sky meets the ground is called the horizon line. In this picture, Loopi shows you the horizon line.

Look closely at the picture of the road. A point shows where the lines on the road come together. The point looks far away in the picture. Follow the lines to the point. Do the lines appear to get closer and closer together as your eyes move toward the point?

Can you find a line that looks like Dash? How does this line appear to change when you follow it to the point on the horizon line?

In this picture, the space above the car is filled with leaves. In the space below the leaves, you can see the ground.

The car looks small because it is far away. The trees that are far away look small, too.

The Lino Brothers help you see space between the trees. Do the trees look closer together when they are far away? Can you see the ground behind the trees? Can you see the sky in the blue space between the leaves?

Ando Hiroshige, *Sunrise,* 1833–1834. Woodblock print on paper.

This is a picture of a Japanese village. The blue space under the boats is water. The white space above the boats shows the clouds. What is the blue space around the clouds?

Can you see the horizon line in this picture? Do the boats look smaller when they are farther away? Do the people look smaller when they are farther away?

Can you find straight lines that look like Loopi?

This is what the earth would look like if you were in a spaceship above the moon. The earth is far away. The moon is close. There is a lot of space between the moon and earth.

Dotty shows you the form of the earth. Where the sun does not shine, you can see a shadow.

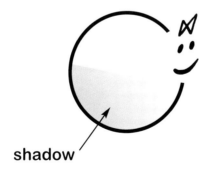

shadow

Look at the picture. What color is the space around the earth's form?

This is a neighborhood in San Francisco. The buildings are very close together. The trees look as if they are on top of each other. Are the trees far apart or close together?

Study the picture of the buildings. Dotty helps you see the top edges of the buildings closest to you. The buildings far away are in the space called the **background.** How do the buildings in the background look different from the buildings closer to you?

The artist Pablo Picasso created this **collage** using paper shapes. He used a blue **rectangle** to make a violin.

When things in a picture look flat, we say the picture is **two-dimensional** or "2-D."

Dotty shows you a page of musical notes. The page is behind the shape that **represents** a violin. Do you see other shapes behind the violin? Can you see the brown space around the shapes?

Left: Pablo Picasso, *Violin with Sheet of Music,* 1912. Paper collage.

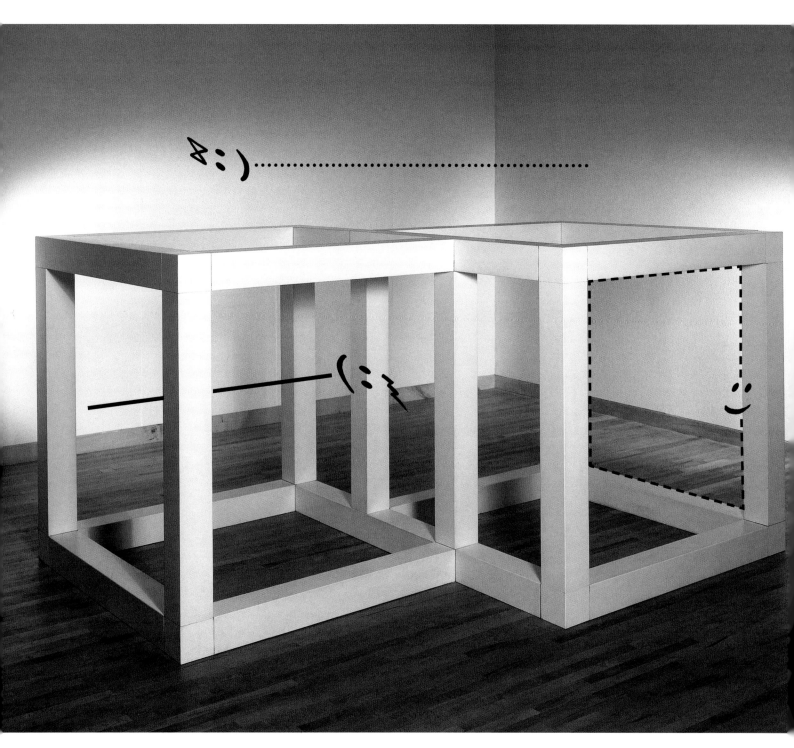

Sol LeWitt, *Two Open Modular Cubes/Half-Off,* 1972. Painted wood.

Some artwork is not flat. You could walk in the space around this sculpture. The things in this picture are **three-dimensional** or "3-D."

Loopi shows you space inside the sculpture.

Dotty shows you space outside the sculpture. Is she above or below the sculpture?

Dash helps you see the space behind the sculpture. What color is the space behind the sculpture? What color is the space under the sculpture?

How many cubes do you see in the picture?

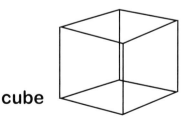

cube

Edward Hopper, *Ryder's House,* 1933. Oil on canvas.

This house was painted by Edward Hopper. He used shapes, color, and shadows to show the form of a house. It does not look flat. It looks 3-D!

Study Edward Hopper's painting. Behind the house, there are plants and hills in the background. The space in front of the house is called the **foreground.** Can you see the green and gold plants in the foreground?

Hopper used shadows to help you see 3-D space in his painting. The picture on this page shows a part of the house. Loopi helps you see the bright side of the house where the sun is shining. The side where the sun does not shine is darker. That side is in the shadow. You can see the house's shadow on the ground. Now look closely at Hopper's painting. Can you see the different shadows in the painting?

Do you see shadows in the background and the foreground?

Does Loopi make the shape of a rectangle? Can you see different shapes in the painting?

shadow

Joseph Jansen, *A View of Chamonix and Mont Blanc*, c. 1860. Oil on canvas.

Joseph Jansen painted this **landscape** of mountains and trees in France. The color of the mountains looks lighter when they are farther away from you. Jansen's painting shows what natural space in the real

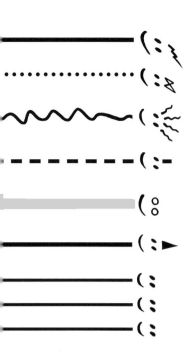

Put It All Together

Take a minute to study the painting by Joseph Jansen. Do you see how the color of the green trees becomes lighter when they are far away? The trees that are far away are smaller, too. Are the houses in the distance different from the house in the foreground? There are many ideas in this painting that can help you create your own landscape.

Make a Collage with Shapes

Do you remember the collage by Pablo Picasso on page 24? You can make a collage by pasting shapes onto paper. You can use different colors and sizes. What did Picasso put in his collage to make you think of music? You can cut out magazine pictures to add to your collage.

Students, Teachers, and Parents

LOOPI the Fantastic Line™ is always waiting to help you learn more about drawing with space—at **www.scribblesinstitute.com**. You can get helpful ideas for your drawings at the Scribbles Institute™. It's a great place for students, teachers, and parents to find books, information, and tips about drawing. You can even get advice from a drawing coach!

The Scribbles Institute™

SCRIBBLESINSTITUTE.COM

31

Glossary

background (BAK-grownd)
The background is the part of a picture that is farthest away from the viewer. It is in back of other things in the scene.

collage (kuh-LAHZH)
A collage is a picture made by pasting things onto a flat surface. You can paste fabric, paper, newspaper, photographs, and other things onto the surface.

foreground (FOR-grownd)
The foreground is the part of a picture that is closest to the viewer. It is in front of other things in the scene.

landscape (LAND-skayp)
A landscape is a picture that shows a view of scenery or the land.

rectangle (REK-tang-ull)
A rectangle is a four-sided shape. Two sides of a rectangle are long, and two sides are short.

represent (rep-reh-ZENT)
To represent something means to show it in a picture. A drawing of a daisy represents the flower.

sculpture (SKULP-cher)
A sculpture is a work of art formed into a shape to represent something. Sculptures can be carved from stone or made from metal.

three-dimensional (THREE dih-MEN-shun-ull)
If an artwork is three-dimensional ("3-D"), it appears to have depth. Three-dimensional objects have length, width, and height.

two-dimensional (TOO dih-MEN-shun-ull)
If an artwork is two-dimensional ("2-D"), it looks flat. Two-dimensional objects only have width and height.

Index

background, 22, 29
cave painting, 9
circle, 9
collage, 24-25, 31
color, 9, 20, 27, 28, 30, 31
cubes, 26-27
Dürer, Albrecht, 12-13
Egypt, 10
foreground, 29
Hopper, Edward, 28-29
horizon line, 14-15, 19
Jansen, Joseph, 30, 31
landscape, 30-31
Picasso, Pablo, 24-25
pyramid, 10-11
rectangle, 25-26, 29
San Francisco, 22-23
sculpture, 12, 26-27
self-portrait, 12-13
shadow, 20-21, 28-29
shape, 9, 25, 28, 29, 31
three-dimensional, 27, 28-29
two-dimensional, 25

About the Author
Rob Court is a designer and illustrator. He has a studio in San Juan Capistrano, California. He started the Scribbles Institute™ to help people learn about the importance of drawing and creativity.

This book is dedicated to Jesse and Jasmine.